BEARDED DRAGON CARE 101

Everything You Need to Keep Your Pet Thriving

Mansa Adzo

Table of Contents

INTRODUCTION

Bearded dragons, often referred to as "beardies," are one of the most popular pet reptiles, loved for their docile nature, easy care, and unique appearance. Native to the deserts of Australia, these fascinating lizards have become favorites among reptile enthusiasts worldwide. Their name comes from the spiny "beard" of scales around their neck, which can puff up when they feel threatened or excited. Bearded dragons are known for their friendly and curious personalities. They tend to be social, enjoying interaction with their owners and even showing affection by sitting on their laps or being hand-fed. With a calm demeanor, they make excellent pets for both beginners and experienced reptile keepers. These reptiles are omnivores, which means they eat a varied diet of insects, vegetables, and fruits. Their ability to thrive on a diverse range of foods makes them relatively easy to care for. Bearded dragons also need specific environmental conditions, such as a warm, dry habitat with appropriate lighting, to mimic their natural desert environment. Whether you're a first-time reptile owner or a seasoned enthusiast, owning a bearded dragon can be a rewarding experience. Their unique behaviors, endearing qualities, and relatively simple care requirements make them an excellent choice for anyone looking to add a reptile to their home.

OVERVIEW OF BEARDED DRAGONS: ORIGINS AND CHARACTERISTICS

Bearded dragons, scientifically known as Pogona vitticeps, are native to the arid regions of central and eastern Australia. These remarkable reptiles are well-adapted to life in the desert, where they bask in the sun and forage for a diet that includes both plants and insects. The species is commonly found in a variety of habitats, such as scrublands, woodlands, and rocky outcrops, making them versatile and resilient creatures.

The name "bearded dragon" refers to the spiny, beard-like scales around their neck. When a bearded dragon feels threatened or excited, it can puff up these scales, creating a dark, intimidating "beard" as a defense mechanism. In addition to their distinctive beard, bearded dragons are known for their triangular heads, robust bodies, and long, whip-like tails. They are relatively small to medium-sized lizards, typically growing to about 18 to 24 inches (45 to 61 cm) in length, including their tail.

Bearded dragons are also famous for their calm and social temperament. Unlike many reptiles, they often enjoy human interaction, and can even become accustomed to handling and affection. In the wild, they are solitary animals, but in captivity, they can adapt to living with other beardies, provided they have enough space.

These reptiles have excellent eyesight and can detect movement from great distances. They also possess unique behaviors, such as "arm waving" or "head bobbing," which are used for communication, often to establish dominance or show submission. In terms of care, bearded dragons are relatively low-maintenance pets, but they do require a warm, dry environment with proper lighting and UVB exposure to stay healthy. Their diet is omnivorous, consisting of insects like crickets and mealworms, as well as leafy greens, vegetables, and fruits. With their striking appearance, gentle nature, and manageable care requirements, bearded dragons have become one of the most popular reptile pets worldwide.

WHY BEARDED DRAGONS MAKE GREAT PETS

Bearded dragons are often considered one of the best reptile pets for both beginners and seasoned reptile enthusiasts. Their unique characteristics, friendly nature, and manageable care requirements make them an excellent choice for anyone looking to add a reptile to their home. Here are some reasons why bearded dragons make great pets:

1. Friendly and Social Nature

Bearded dragons are known for their calm and social demeanor. Unlike many other reptiles that prefer solitude, beardies tend to enjoy interaction with their owners. They can become very accustomed to human presence, and some even show affection by sitting on their owner's lap or following them around their enclosure. With regular handling, they can develop strong bonds with their owners, making them rewarding companions.

2. Easy to Care For

Compared to many other exotic pets, bearded dragons have relatively simple care needs. They thrive in a well-maintained environment with the right temperature, lighting, and humidity levels. With a proper setup—such as a spacious terrarium with heat lamps and UVB lighting—they can live comfortably. Their omnivorous diet is also relatively easy to manage, as they eat a variety of insects, vegetables, and fruits, making feeding both affordable and straightforward.

3. Low Maintenance

Bearded dragons don't require constant attention, making them a great pet for people with busy schedules. They are generally independent but enjoy interaction when their owners are available. Unlike some pets that need regular grooming, bearded dragons are low-maintenance in terms of hygiene, aside from periodic tank cleaning.

4. Interactive and Entertaining

Bearded dragons are known for their quirky behaviors that can be both entertaining and endearing. They often engage in fascinating activities like "head bobbing" and "arm waving," which they use to communicate with other dragons or to display dominance. Watching these unique behaviors can be a source of enjoyment for their owners.

5. Long Lifespan

Bearded dragons have a relatively long lifespan for a reptile. With proper care, they can live up to 10-15 years or more, allowing owners to form a long-lasting bond with their pet. This makes them a good investment for those seeking a companion that will be with them for many years.

6. Non-Aggressive and Easy to Handle

One of the key reasons bearded dragons are so popular is their gentle temperament. They are rarely aggressive and are usually tolerant of being handled. When treated with respect and given time to adjust, bearded dragons can become very comfortable with their owners, making them ideal pets for families and individuals alike.

7. Space-Efficient

While bearded dragons do need space to roam and explore, they don't require the same vast enclosures as some other reptiles. A well-sized terrarium with appropriate climbing structures and hiding spots is enough to provide them with a comfortable home. This makes them suitable for people living in apartments or homes with limited space.

8. Great for Learning

For young reptile enthusiasts, bearded dragons are an excellent way to learn about reptile care and responsibility. Their manageable size and easygoing nature provide a hands-on opportunity to teach children about animal care and respect for living creatures.

In summary, bearded dragons are an ideal choice for people looking for a friendly, easy-to-care-for, and engaging pet. Their unique personalities, long lifespan, and ability to bond with their owners make them a standout choice among reptiles. Whether you're a first-time pet owner or an experienced reptile keeper, a bearded dragon is sure to bring joy and companionship to your home.

UNDERSTANDING BEARDED DRAGON BEHAVIOR AND TEMPERAMENT

Bearded dragons are known for their calm and friendly nature, making them one of the most popular pet reptiles. However, like any animal, they have their own set of behaviors and temperaments that are important to understand in order to provide the best care. Knowing how they communicate, react to their environment, and express emotions can help you foster a positive relationship with your pet. Here's an overview of bearded dragon behavior and temperament:

1. Docile and Friendly

One of the main reasons bearded dragons make great pets is their docile temperament. Unlike many other reptiles, bearded dragons are naturally curious and enjoy interaction with their owners. They can become accustomed to handling and even form bonds with their human caretakers. With gentle, regular handling, bearded dragons typically remain calm and tolerant, making them ideal pets for families and first-time reptile owners.

2. Body Language: Arm Waving and Head Bobbing

Bearded dragons communicate using various body language signals, including arm waving and head bobbing. These behaviors are essential to understanding their mood and intentions:

• Arm Waving: This is often seen in younger bearded dragons and is a sign of submission or recognition. When they wave one of their arms in a circular motion, they are signaling that they are not a threat and are acknowledging the dominance of another dragon or human. It's a peaceful gesture and not an indication of aggression.

• Head Bobbing: Bearded dragons frequently bob their heads, especially when establishing dominance. Male dragons are more likely to perform this behavior, especially when competing with other males. However, head bobbing can also be a sign of excitement or territorial behavior. In some cases, a female may bob her head in response to a male's courtship display.

3. Beard Puffing and Color Changes

A bearded dragon's "beard" is the spiny flap of skin that wraps around its neck. When the dragon feels threatened, stressed, or excited, it can puff out this beard, often turning it dark in color. This display is a defensive mechanism to make the dragon appear larger and more intimidating. Additionally, their body color may change depending on their mood or environmental conditions. Bearded dragons may darken their skin when they are angry, stressed, or feeling cold. Conversely, they might lighten up or show brighter colors when they are basking in warmth and feeling relaxed.

4. Exploring and Curiosity

Bearded dragons are naturally curious creatures, especially when introduced to new environments or objects. They will often explore their surroundings, climbing on rocks, branches, and any other accessible surfaces in their enclosure. This behavior is instinctive, as they are naturally foragers and explorers in the wild. Providing them with enrichment in the form of climbing structures and hide spots will satisfy their curiosity and keep them mentally stimulated.

5. Hunting and Feeding Behavior

As omnivores, bearded dragons have a varied diet that includes both plant matter and insects. They are active hunters and will often chase and catch insects, especially crickets, mealworms, and other small creatures. When feeding, bearded dragons may demonstrate hunting behaviors like stalking or pouncing. They may also "taste" or lick new food items before eating them. Understanding their feeding behavior is key to maintaining a healthy diet for your pet, as a mix of protein and vegetables is essential for their nutrition.

6. Territorial Behavior

Bearded dragons can exhibit territorial behaviors, particularly if they feel their space is being invaded. This is common in male dragons, especially when housed with other males. Territorial behaviors can include head bobbing, puffing out their beard, and displaying aggression through hissing or lunging. It's important to ensure that their enclosure is spacious enough to avoid conflict if you have multiple bearded dragons. If you notice signs of aggression, separating them and giving each one its own space can help alleviate tension.

7. Brumation (Seasonal Dormancy)

Bearded dragons may enter a state of brumation, similar to hibernation, during the cooler months, usually in the winter. During brumation, they become less active, eat less, and may sleep for extended periods of time. This behavior is natural and not necessarily a sign of illness, although it's important to ensure that their habitat is still appropriately warm and well-lit. If your bearded dragon stops eating or seems lethargic for an extended period, it's best to consult a vet to rule out any health issues.

8. Signs of Stress or Discomfort

While bearded dragons are generally tolerant and calm, they can become stressed if their environment is not ideal. Signs of stress may include excessive hiding, glass surfing (when the dragon repeatedly bangs against the sides of the enclosure), loss of appetite, or aggression. Common stress triggers include improper temperatures, lack of hiding spaces, inadequate lighting, or overhandling. It's important to observe your bearded dragon's behavior and make adjustments to its care routine as needed to maintain a healthy and happy pet.

9. Affectionate Behavior

Although reptiles are often perceived as cold and aloof, bearded dragons can show affection toward their owners. Many beardies enjoy being held and will actively seek out human interaction. They may even tolerate sitting on your shoulder or lap, where they can rest comfortably while observing their surroundings. With gentle handling and positive reinforcement, bearded dragons can become quite affectionate and form strong bonds with their human caretakers.

Understanding bearded dragon behavior and temperament is key to fostering a positive relationship with your pet. Their docile nature, unique communication methods, and natural curiosity make them fascinating and interactive companions. By paying attention to their body language, environment, and needs, you can ensure a happy and healthy life for your bearded dragon.

CHAPTER ONE

WHAT YOU NEED TO KNOW BEFORE GETTING A BEARDED DRAGON

Bearded dragons are wonderful pets, but before bringing one into your home, it's important to understand their needs and what it takes to care for them properly. These reptiles require specific environments, diets, and attention to thrive, and being well-prepared will ensure a happy and healthy relationship with your new pet. Here's what you need to know before getting a bearded dragon:

1. Commitment and Lifespan

Bearded dragons can live for 10 to 15 years or more with proper care. This long lifespan means you'll be committing to caring for your pet for a decade or more. Before getting a bearded dragon, make sure you're prepared for this long-term commitment in terms of time, energy, and resources.

2. Proper Habitat Setup

A bearded dragon's enclosure is crucial to its well-being. You will need to create a habitat that mimics its natural desert environment. Here are the key elements to consider:

• Tank Size: Bearded dragons need plenty of space to move around. A 40-gallon tank is typically the minimum size for an adult bearded dragon, though larger enclosures are better, especially for active dragons.

• Heating and Lighting: Since bearded dragons are cold-blooded, they rely on external heat sources to regulate their body temperature. You'll need a heat lamp to maintain a basking area temperature of 95°F to 110°F (35°C to 43°C) and a cooler side of the tank that is around 75°F to 85°F (24°C to 29°C). Additionally, a UVB light is essential to help them synthesize vitamin D3, which is needed to absorb calcium and prevent metabolic bone disease.

• Substrate: The floor of the tank should be lined with a safe substrate. Avoid using loose sand, which can cause impaction if ingested, and instead opt for reptile carpet, tiles, or paper towels.

3. Dietary Needs

Bearded dragons are omnivores, meaning they eat both plant matter and animal protein. Their diet should be well-balanced, with a mix of:

• Insects: Crickets, mealworms, dubia roaches, and other insects make up a large part of their diet, especially for younger dragons. Make sure the insects are appropriately sized for your dragon to avoid choking hazards.

• Vegetables and Fruits: Offer a variety of leafy greens (like collard greens, mustard greens, and dandelion greens) and vegetables (such as squash, bell peppers, and carrots). Fruits like berries, melon, and apples can be given as occasional treats but should not make up more than 10-20% of their diet.

• Supplements: Bearded dragons need calcium and vitamin D3 supplements to support their bone health. Dusting their food with a calcium supplement is essential, especially for young dragons and females that are laying eggs.

4. Temperament and Handling

Bearded dragons are generally docile and easy to handle, but it's important to understand their temperament:

• Social Interaction: Bearded dragons enjoy human interaction and can become very affectionate, often seeking out attention and sitting on their owners' laps. However, they are not as social as some other pets and may need some time to adjust to handling, especially if they are not used to it.

• Handling with Care: Always handle your bearded dragon gently. It's best to scoop them up from underneath their belly, supporting their body and avoiding any sudden movements. Overhandling or rough treatment can lead to stress.

5. Health Care and Vet Visits

Like any pet, bearded dragons need regular health check-ups. While they are relatively low-maintenance, they are prone to some health issues, including:

• Metabolic Bone Disease: This can be caused by insufficient UVB light or calcium deficiency. Regularly monitor their diet and UVB exposure to prevent this condition.

• Parasites: Bearded dragons are prone to intestinal parasites. Regular fecal tests and deworming (if necessary) can help maintain their health.

• Shedding Issues: Bearded dragons shed their skin as they grow, and they may need help shedding in certain areas. Ensure the environment has appropriate humidity levels to help with the shedding process.

6. Temperature and Humidity Control

Maintaining the proper temperature and humidity levels is crucial for your bearded dragon's health. While they thrive in dry, desert-like conditions, they do need a temperature gradient in their enclosure. The basking area should be hot (95°F to 110°F), while the cooler side of the tank should be around 75°F to 85°F. Humidity should be kept low, around 30% to 40%, as high humidity can lead to respiratory problems. A hygrometer (humidity gauge) and thermometer are essential tools to monitor these conditions.

7. Time and Attention

Although bearded dragons are relatively low-maintenance pets, they still require attention and regular care. They need daily feeding, cleaning of their enclosure, and monitoring of their health and environment. Additionally, they benefit from time outside of their enclosure for supervised exploration and interaction with their owners.

8. Potential Allergies or Sensitivities

Bearded dragons may have allergic reactions to certain foods or materials. Always monitor them for signs of allergic reactions like swelling or digestive upset after introducing new foods or changes in their environment. It's important to avoid foods that are toxic to reptiles, such as avocado, onions, and certain types of citrus.

9. Living Arrangements

Before getting a bearded dragon, ensure that your living space is suitable for a large tank. Bearded dragons need a lot of space to move around and a stable, warm environment. Keep in mind that their enclosures are quite large, and they will need a place where they can get plenty of natural light or have their UVB light source in the tank for 10-12 hours a day.

10. Cost and Maintenance

Bearded dragons are not inexpensive pets. The initial setup for their habitat, including the tank, lighting, heating, and decor, can be costly. In addition, you will need to regularly purchase food, supplements, and replacement bulbs for their lights. Regular veterinary care, particularly for new or young bearded dragons, adds to the cost of ownership.

Before getting a bearded dragon, it's essential to understand their care requirements, the time and attention they need, and the long-term commitment involved. With the right habitat, diet, and care, bearded dragons make fantastic pets that are interactive, low-maintenance, and rewarding to keep. By preparing ahead of time, you'll be able to provide a happy, healthy life for your bearded dragon and enjoy many years of companionship.

SETTING UP THE PERFECT HABITAT FOR YOUR BEARDED DRAGON

Creating the ideal habitat for your bearded dragon is essential to its health and well-being. Bearded dragons are native to the arid deserts of Australia, so their environment should mimic those conditions, including appropriate temperature, lighting, and space. Below is a guide to setting up the perfect habitat to keep your bearded dragon healthy, happy, and comfortable.

1. Choosing the Right Enclosure Size and Type

The first step in setting up a suitable home for your bearded dragon is selecting the right enclosure. Bearded dragons need space to roam, climb, and bask, so it's essential to choose a tank that accommodates their size and activity level.

• Size: For an adult bearded dragon, a minimum of a 40-gallon tank is recommended, though larger is always better. A 75-gallon or 120-gallon tank provides more space for your dragon to move around. Hatchlings and juveniles can live in smaller enclosures but will need to be upgraded as they grow.

• Type of Tank: A glass aquarium is the most common and widely available enclosure for bearded dragons. It's easy to clean, provides visibility, and allows for proper heat and lighting setups. Ensure that the tank has a secure, well-ventilated lid to prevent escapes.

• Vertical Space: Bearded dragons are natural climbers, so a tank with both horizontal and vertical space is ideal. Ensure that your enclosure has room for climbing structures, such as rocks, branches, and logs.

2. Creating a Comfortable and Safe Environment

In addition to space, the safety and comfort of your bearded dragon depend on the setup of its environment.

• Temperature Gradient: Bearded dragons need a temperature gradient to regulate their body temperature. The basking area should be between 95°F and 110°F (35°C - 43°C) during the day, while the cooler side of the enclosure should be between 75°F and 85°F (24°C - 29°C). This allows the dragon to move between warm and cool areas depending on its needs. Use thermometers to monitor both the basking and cool sides of the enclosure.

• Humidity: Bearded dragons come from dry, arid environments, so the humidity in their habitat should be kept low, between 30% and 40%. High humidity levels can cause respiratory issues. Use a hygrometer to monitor the humidity, and avoid misting the enclosure unless it's during shedding to help with skin sloughing.

• Ventilation: Proper airflow is important to avoid excess humidity buildup and prevent bacterial growth. Make sure the enclosure is well-ventilated, with sufficient openings in the lid or sides.

3. Lighting and Heating: UVB, Basking, and Night Temperature

Proper lighting and heating are critical to the health of your bearded dragon. Without the right lighting, your dragon may suffer from nutritional deficiencies and stress.

• UVB Lighting: Bearded dragons need UVB light to synthesize vitamin D3, which is crucial for calcium absorption and overall bone health. Use a UVB fluorescent bulb that covers the length of the tank. UVB bulbs should be replaced every 6 months, as their intensity decreases over time. Ensure the UVB light is positioned 8-12 inches from the basking spot.

• Basking Light: Bearded dragons need a basking light to create a warm spot in their enclosure. A basking bulb should provide the appropriate temperature range (95°F to 110°F) and create a hotspot for your dragon to thermoregulate. You can use incandescent or halogen bulbs for basking. Ensure that the basking light is positioned at one end of the tank to create a gradient.

• Night Temperature: Bearded dragons do not require heat at night but need to maintain a temperature between 65°F and 75°F (18°C to 24°C). A drop in temperature at night mimics the desert's natural cycle. If needed, use a ceramic heat emitter or a low-wattage red or blue bulb at night to maintain warmth without disturbing their sleep.

• Timers: Use a timer to regulate the lighting. Bearded dragons need around 10-12 hours of light during the day and 12-14 hours of darkness at night. This cycle helps them establish a natural day/night rhythm.

4. Substrates: Choosing the Best Flooring for Your Bearded Dragon

The substrate is the material used to line the bottom of the enclosure, and it serves both practical and aesthetic purposes. The right substrate ensures comfort and ease of cleaning while preventing health issues.

• Best Options:

Reptile Carpet: This is a safe, non-impactive substrate that is easy to clean and soft on your bearded dragon's feet. It's a great choice for bearded dragons, as they won't accidentally ingest it.

Tiles: Ceramic or slate tiles make an excellent substrate because they are easy to clean, allow for natural digging behavior, and won't be ingested. Tiles also help regulate the temperature and can mimic natural desert surfaces.

Paper Towels or Butcher Paper: These are budget-friendly and easy to replace. While they don't allow for natural behaviors like digging, they are practical for hatchlings and juveniles, who can be more prone to ingesting loose substrate.

• Avoid Loose Substrates: Sand, gravel, and soil should be avoided, especially for young dragons, as they are more likely to ingest it, which can lead to impaction, a potentially deadly condition.

5. Decorations, Hiding Spots, and Enrichment Ideas

Decorations and enrichment items make your bearded dragon's habitat more interesting and provide them with opportunities to exhibit natural behaviors.

• Climbing Structures: Bearded dragons are natural climbers, so providing rocks, branches, and logs is essential for their physical health and mental stimulation. Ensure that the decorations are securely placed and won't topple over, as bearded dragons like to climb and perch on them.

• Hiding Spots: Bearded dragons need places to retreat to for privacy and security. Provide caves, hollow logs, or small shelters where your dragon can hide if it feels stressed, threatened, or needs to rest. Hiding spots also help simulate their natural environment, where they can escape the heat of the day and find cool, shaded areas.

• Enrichment: Bearded dragons benefit from mental stimulation. Changing the layout of their habitat occasionally, adding live plants, or offering them new objects to interact with (such as cardboard boxes or new climbing structures) can keep them engaged. Additionally, allowing them supervised out-of-tank time for exploration can enhance their quality of life.

• Plants: You can add safe, non-toxic plants to the enclosure to mimic a natural environment. Some suitable plants for bearded dragon enclosures include pothos, hibiscus, and spider plants. Be sure the plants you add are safe and non-toxic, as some common plants can be harmful to reptiles.

Setting up the perfect habitat for your bearded dragon requires careful consideration of its space, temperature, lighting, substrate, and enrichment. By providing the right environment, you'll ensure that your bearded dragon can thrive, stay healthy, and feel comfortable in its home. Regularly monitor the conditions in the enclosure to make any necessary adjustments, and remember that a little effort in creating the right habitat will lead to a happy and thriving pet.

BEARDED DRAGON HEALTH AND WELL-BEING

Ensuring that your bearded dragon remains healthy and comfortable is one of the most important aspects of being a responsible pet owner. A well-maintained habitat, proper diet, and regular care can prevent many common health issues. In this section, we'll discuss the signs of a healthy bearded dragon, common health problems and preventative care, how to deal with parasites and infections, and essential first aid knowledge.

1. Signs of a Healthy Bearded Dragon

A healthy bearded dragon will display certain behaviors and physical characteristics that indicate it is in good condition. Here's what to look for:

• Active and Alert: A healthy bearded dragon will be alert, responsive to stimuli, and active, especially during the day when they are most active. They should show curiosity, move around their enclosure, and bask regularly.

• Bright Eyes: Healthy bearded dragons have clear, bright eyes with no discharge or swelling. They should not appear sunken or dull.

• Healthy Skin: The skin should be smooth, without signs of excessive shedding or sores. Some shedding is normal, but it should occur in patches, not in large chunks.

• Healthy Appetite: A good appetite is a key sign of health. Bearded dragons typically eat a combination of insects and vegetables. A drop in appetite can indicate health problems.

• Normal Stool: Healthy dragons produce firm, dark stools with little to no odor. Abnormal stool or frequent diarrhea can be a sign of digestive issues or parasites.

• Breathing: Bearded dragons should breathe easily without wheezing or other signs of respiratory distress.

2. Common Health Issues and Preventative Care

Like all reptiles, bearded dragons are susceptible to certain health conditions. The best way to address these issues is through regular care, proper habitat maintenance, and preventive measures.

• Metabolic Bone Disease (MBD): MBD occurs when a bearded dragon's bones become soft and deformed due to a lack of calcium and UVB light. To prevent MBD, provide UVB lighting, a proper calcium supplement, and a balanced diet.

• Respiratory Infections: Respiratory issues, such as wheezing, labored breathing, or discharge from the nose, are often caused by poor environmental conditions, such as high humidity or insufficient heating. Ensure that the habitat has the correct temperature gradient and humidity levels.

• Parasites: Bearded dragons can suffer from internal parasites such as pinworms, coccidia, and Giardia, which can cause weight loss, diarrhea, or lethargy. Regular vet check-ups and proper hygiene can help prevent parasites.

• Obesity: Overfeeding, particularly of high-fat foods like certain insects, can lead to obesity. Maintain a balanced diet with appropriate portions to avoid this condition.

• Dehydration: Lack of hydration can lead to lethargy, dry skin, and sunken eyes. Ensure your bearded dragon has access to fresh water daily and is bathed regularly to promote hydration.

3. Dealing with Mites, Parasites, and Infections

Bearded dragons are prone to certain external and internal health issues. Knowing how to recognize and address them promptly is vital.

• Mites: Mites are tiny external parasites that can infest a bearded dragon's skin. They often cause itching, irritation, and a loss of skin color. If you notice tiny black or red specks on your dragon's body, it may have mites. Mite treatments include specialized baths and enclosure cleaning, but always consult a veterinarian for advice.

• Internal Parasites: As mentioned, internal parasites can cause digestive issues such as diarrhea, weight loss, and lethargy. If you suspect your bearded dragon has parasites, it's important to take a stool sample to your vet for analysis. A deworming treatment may be necessary, as well as adjustments to their diet or environment.

• Fungal Infections: Fungal infections are another concern, particularly if the environment is too humid. Symptoms include skin lesions, changes in color, or a rough, flaky texture to the skin. If suspected, visit a vet who can prescribe appropriate antifungal treatments.

• Bacterial Infections: Bearded dragons are prone to bacterial infections, especially if there are open wounds or cuts. Common bacterial infections may cause swelling, redness, or pus around the affected area. Prompt vet intervention is necessary to treat infections with antibiotics.

4. Bearded Dragon First Aid: What Every Owner Should Know

In case of an emergency, it's essential for bearded dragon owners to know basic first aid procedures. Here are some essential tips:

• Handling Burns: If your bearded dragon gets burned from an overheat basking light, immediately remove it from the heat source. Clean the burn area with lukewarm water and apply a cooling, antiseptic ointment. Seek veterinary help if the burn is severe.

• Cuts or Scrapes: If your bearded dragon has a cut or scrape, gently clean the wound with saline solution or a reptile-safe antiseptic. Apply an antibiotic ointment to prevent infection. If the wound is deep, it's best to see a vet.

• Signs of Impaction: Impaction is a common condition caused by ingesting unsuitable materials (such as substrate or large prey) that block the digestive tract. Signs of impaction include loss of appetite, lethargy, and difficulty defecating. If you suspect impaction, take your bearded dragon to the vet for diagnosis and possible treatment, such as warm baths or medication.

• Heat Stroke: If a bearded dragon is exposed to excessive heat, it can suffer from heatstroke. Symptoms include lethargy, excessive panting, or a glassy-eyed appearance. To treat heatstroke, move your dragon to a cooler area, and provide water to drink. If symptoms persist, see a vet immediately.

5. Regular Checkups and Vet Visits: When and Why

Bearded dragons benefit from regular checkups to ensure their health is on track and to catch potential issues early. Regular veterinary visits are essential, particularly if your bearded dragon shows any signs of illness or has specific health concerns.

• Initial Vet Visit: When you first acquire your bearded dragon, it's a good idea to schedule an initial health checkup with an experienced reptile vet. The vet can check for common health issues and provide advice on proper care.

• Annual Checkups: Even if your bearded dragon seems healthy, a yearly checkup is recommended. The vet will perform a physical examination and may recommend fecal testing for parasites, especially if your dragon is showing any signs of illness.

• When to See a Vet: Take your bearded dragon to the vet if you notice any of the following symptoms:

Loss of appetite

Lethargy or unusual inactivity

Changes in stool (diarrhea, mucus, or blood)

Difficulty breathing or wheezing

Swollen limbs or unusual skin lesions

Changes in behavior (such as hiding excessively)

By being proactive and attentive to your bearded dragon's health, you can ensure that it remains happy and well for many years. Regular habitat maintenance, a balanced diet, and monitoring for signs of illness are all part of responsible pet ownership. Should any health issues arise, prompt action and veterinary care are crucial for ensuring your dragon's long-term well-being.

CHAPTER TWO

FEEDING YOUR BEARDED DRAGON

Proper nutrition is essential to the health and longevity of your bearded dragon. As omnivores, they require a balanced diet consisting of both animal protein and plant-based foods. Understanding what, how, and how often to feed your bearded dragon is key to providing a healthy and happy life.

1. Understanding Bearded Dragon Diet: Omnivore Needs

Bearded dragons are omnivores, meaning they eat both animal and plant-based foods. This gives them a diverse diet that helps ensure they get the right nutrients for growth, energy, and overall health. Their diet consists primarily of:

• Insects: Bearded dragons enjoy live insects like crickets, dubia roaches, mealworms, and superworms, which provide essential protein and fats.

• Vegetables: Leafy greens, such as collard greens, dandelion greens, mustard greens, and turnip greens, are important for their health. They also benefit from other vegetables like squash, bell peppers, and sweet potatoes.

• Fruits: Fruits like strawberries, blueberries, melons, and apples can be offered in moderation, as they are high in sugar and should not make up a large portion of the diet.

While bearded dragons are omnivores, the balance between insects and plants in their diet depends on their age. Juveniles need more protein for growth, while adults benefit from a greater emphasis on vegetables.

2. How to Feed Bearded Dragons: Portion Sizes and Frequency

Bearded dragons have different nutritional needs at various stages of their life. Here's a guideline to ensure you're feeding your pet the right amount:

• Juveniles (0-6 months): Juvenile bearded dragons are growing rapidly and require more protein. Their diet should consist of 60-70% insects and 30-40% vegetables. They should be fed 2-3 times per day with a variety of insects and fresh greens. It's important to offer as many insects as they can eat in a 10-15 minute period, allowing them to build muscle and develop properly.

• Subadults (6-18 months): As your bearded dragon matures, you can start to shift their diet to be more plant-based. Insects should make up 40-50% of their diet, and vegetables should make up

50-60%. Feed them once or twice per day, depending on their activity and appetite.

• Adults (18 months and older): Adult bearded dragons typically need less protein and more fiber. Their diet should consist of 20-30% insects and 70-80% vegetables. You can feed them once a day, with an emphasis on leafy greens and vegetables, while offering insects only 3-4 times a week.

3. Feeding Vegetables, Fruits, and Insects

When it comes to feeding your bearded dragon, variety is essential to ensure they get all the necessary nutrients. Here's a breakdown of the types of foods you should offer:

• Vegetables: Offer a variety of dark leafy greens, such as:

Collard greens

Mustard greens

Dandelion greens

Turnip greens

Kale (in moderation)

You can also feed vegetables like:

Squash (butternut, acorn)

Bell peppers (any color)

Sweet potatoes (cooked)

Carrots (finely chopped)

Zucchini

Avoid feeding bearded dragons high-oxalate vegetables (such as spinach) in large quantities, as oxalates can bind to calcium and reduce its absorption.

• Fruits: Offer fruit in moderation because it's high in sugar. Some good choices include:

Strawberries

Blueberries

Grapes (cut in halves or quarters)

Apples (with seeds removed)

Watermelon

Mango

Fruits are more of a treat and should not make up more than 10-15% of the diet.

• Insects: Insects provide essential protein and fat for your bearded dragon. Some safe options include:

Crickets (avoid too many, as they may carry parasites)

Dubia roaches (a healthy option)

Mealworms (occasionally, but should not be fed too often)

Superworms (high in fat, should be given sparingly)

Phoenix worms (a good choice for calcium)

Gut-loading the insects (feeding them nutritious food before offering them to your dragon) is important for providing your bearded dragon with the most nutrients possible.

4. Supplements and Vitamins: What's Necessary?

Bearded dragons require a variety of nutrients, and sometimes their diet alone may not provide everything they need. Here are the supplements and vitamins that can help ensure your dragon is getting a balanced diet:

• Calcium: Calcium supplementation is critical for bearded dragons, especially for preventing Metabolic Bone Disease (MBD). Sprinkle a calcium supplement on the insects 2-3 times per week for juveniles and at least once a week for adults. It's best to use a calcium supplement without vitamin D3 unless your dragon is not exposed to UVB light, as excessive vitamin D3 can lead to toxicity.

• Vitamin D3: Vitamin D3 helps with calcium absorption. If your bearded dragon receives sufficient UVB light, they may not need additional vitamin D3. However, if they are not getting enough natural sunlight or UVB light from their enclosure, a supplement may be necessary. Use a supplement with vitamin D3 sparingly and in combination with UVB exposure.

• Multivitamins: A multivitamin supplement should be used once a week to ensure your dragon is getting other essential vitamins. Bearded dragons need a range of vitamins, including A, C, and E, but over-supplementing can be harmful. A reptile-specific multivitamin should be used, and it's important to follow the recommended dosage on the packaging.

5. Hydration: Ensuring Proper Water Intake

Bearded dragons, like all reptiles, need adequate hydration to stay healthy. Although they get some moisture from their food, it's important to provide fresh water in their enclosure at all times. Here's how to make sure your bearded dragon stays hydrated:

• Water Dish: Offer a shallow water dish that is easy for your bearded dragon to access. Ensure that the dish is changed daily to prevent bacteria build-up. Bearded dragons may not drink directly from the dish as frequently as other reptiles, but it's still important to keep water available at all times.

• Bathing: Some bearded dragons enjoy being soaked in lukewarm water, which can help with hydration and shedding. Bathing your dragon once or twice a week can also encourage them to drink more. Just be sure not to leave them unattended in water, as they can drown if the water level is too high.

• Mist the Enclosure: Lightly misting the enclosure can increase humidity slightly, which can be beneficial for hydration, particularly during shedding periods. However, you should avoid making the habitat too humid, as this can lead to respiratory issues. Feeding your bearded dragon a balanced diet that includes a variety of insects, vegetables, fruits, and supplements is crucial for their well-being. By providing the right portion sizes, frequency of feeding, and appropriate hydration, you can ensure your pet remains healthy and active. Regularly offering a mix of foods and monitoring your dragon's health will help them live a long, happy life.

UNDERSTANDING BEARDED DRAGON BEHAVIOR

Bearded dragons are unique and fascinating pets with distinct behaviors that can provide insight into their mood, health, and needs. Understanding their body language, common behaviors, and how to socialize with them can help ensure a positive and harmonious relationship with your pet.

1. Decoding Bearded Dragon Body Language

Bearded dragons use various forms of body language to communicate, and recognizing these cues can help you understand how they are feeling. Here are some common body language signs to watch for:

• Beard Puffing: When a bearded dragon puffs out its "beard" (the flap of skin beneath its chin), it is often a sign of aggression or territorial behavior. However, it can also occur when a dragon feels threatened or stressed. A puffed beard can be a defensive reaction, especially when they encounter unfamiliar animals or situations.

• Head Bobbing: This is a common sign of dominance or communication. Male bearded dragons often bob their heads up and down as a way of asserting their territory or challenging another male. Female dragons may also head-bob, but they usually do so in a more subdued manner. When a dragon bobs its head while interacting with a human, it's typically not aggressive but rather a sign of curiosity or acknowledgment.

• Arm Waving: When a bearded dragon raises one of its front legs and waves it in a circular motion, it's a gesture of submission. This behavior is more common in juvenile dragons or in response to a dominant dragon. It is a non-aggressive behavior used to communicate peace and avoid conflict.

• Flattening Body: When a bearded dragon flattens its body and stretches out, it can indicate that they are feeling threatened, scared, or trying to appear larger to intimidate a potential threat. This behavior is often seen when they feel cornered or are facing a perceived danger.

• Tail Wagging: Some bearded dragons will wag their tails, similar to a dog. This can be a sign of excitement, frustration, or even a form of aggression. Pay attention to the context to interpret this behavior correctly.

• Mouth Gaping: Bearded dragons may open their mouths wide to cool down, especially after basking. However, if they are gaping excessively or in other situations, it could be a sign of stress, respiratory infection, or overheating. It's important to monitor this behavior to ensure your dragon is healthy.

2. Common Behavioral Traits and What They Mean

Understanding common behavioral traits can give you a better sense of how your bearded dragon interacts with its environment:

• Exploration and Curiosity: Bearded dragons are naturally curious and enjoy exploring their surroundings. They may climb, burrow, or investigate their habitat to find food or secure hiding spots. This is a healthy and natural behavior, so make sure their environment offers plenty of opportunities for exploration.

• Basking Behavior: Bearded dragons are cold-blooded reptiles that rely on external heat sources to regulate their body temperature. You will often see your dragon basking under a heat source like a basking light. This behavior helps them maintain optimal body temperature for digestion and overall health.

• Shedding: Shedding is a natural and regular process for bearded dragons as they grow. You may notice them scratching against surfaces or rubbing their faces to help peel off the old skin. A healthy dragon will shed in patches, but if shedding is incomplete or excessive, it may indicate health issues like skin infections or dehydration.

• Digging and Hiding: Bearded dragons sometimes dig in their enclosures, especially females, who may dig to lay eggs. If you notice your dragon frequently digging, it could also be a sign that they are stressed, anxious, or trying to find a cool or hidden spot for comfort.

• Grumpiness or Lethargy: If your bearded dragon is acting unusually lethargic, grumpy, or refusing food, it could be an indication of stress, illness, or an improper environment. It's essential to monitor their behavior and consult a vet if necessary.

3. How to Build Trust and Bond with Your Pet

Building trust with your bearded dragon is a gradual process that requires patience and consistency. Here are some tips for forming a bond:

• Consistent Interaction: Spend time with your bearded dragon every day, even if it's just for a few minutes. Handle them gently, allowing them to explore your hands and arms without forcing them into any situation they're uncomfortable with. Over time, your dragon will learn that you're a safe presence.

• Positive Reinforcement: Bearded dragons are intelligent and can associate certain actions with rewards. When your dragon exhibits calm and friendly behavior, offer them a treat or simply praise them with a gentle voice. This positive reinforcement helps them associate your presence with good things.

• Gentle Handling: When you first start handling your bearded dragon, be sure to support their body fully. Avoid grabbing or holding them too tightly, as this can stress them out. Place them on a flat, safe surface like your lap or a soft towel and let them explore at their own pace.

• Time and Patience: Each bearded dragon is different, and it may take time for them to become comfortable with you. Some may take longer to trust people, while others may warm up quickly. Be patient and allow them to adjust at their own pace.

4. Handling and Socializing Your Bearded Dragon

Bearded dragons are generally social creatures that enjoy interacting with their owners. However, they can also be sensitive to their environment and may need time to adjust to new people or situations. Here's how to handle and socialize your bearded dragon effectively:

• Slow Introductions: When introducing your bearded dragon to new people or pets, take it slow. Start with brief interactions, allowing your dragon to become accustomed to different smells, sounds, and sights. Gradually increase the length and frequency of these sessions as your dragon becomes more confident.

• Respect Their Space: Just like people, bearded dragons need their personal space. Avoid picking them up or handling them when they are basking or hiding, as this may cause stress. Instead, handle them when they are more alert and active.

• Socializing with Other Pets: Bearded dragons can be socialized with other reptiles and animals, but it's crucial to monitor their interactions carefully. They should never be housed with other bearded dragons unless they are of similar size and temperament to avoid territorial disputes or aggression.

5. Avoiding Stress and Aggression

Stress and aggression are common issues with bearded dragons, but they can often be avoided by creating the right environment and handling them properly:

• Proper Habitat: Make sure the enclosure is large enough to accommodate your bearded dragon's size and that it includes both warm and cool areas for them to regulate their temperature. A well-designed habitat will help your dragon feel secure and reduce stress.

• Avoid Overhandling: While it's important to socialize your dragon, excessive handling can lead to stress. Limit the amount of time you handle them, especially during shedding or when they are settling into a new environment.

• Respecting Their Boundaries: Pay attention to body language cues. If your bearded dragon is displaying signs of stress (like head bobbing, tail wagging, or puffing out their beard), give them some space to calm down.

• Consistent Routine: Bearded dragons thrive on routine. Try to feed, handle, and clean their enclosure at the same times each day. This predictability will help reduce stress and make them feel more secure. Understanding your bearded dragon's behavior and body language is essential for building a trusting and positive relationship. By paying attention to their cues, being patient, and handling them properly, you can ensure that your bearded dragon is a happy, healthy, and well-adjusted companion.

BEARDED DRAGON GROWTH AND DEVELOPMENT

Bearded dragons go through distinct stages of growth, from hatching as tiny creatures to becoming fully grown adults. Understanding these stages, growth milestones, and how to care for your dragon during each phase is crucial to ensuring a healthy and happy pet. Additionally, addressing common issues such as molting and obesity can help manage their growth and development effectively.

1. Life Stages: Hatchling, Juvenile, and Adult

Bearded dragons undergo significant changes as they grow. Each life stage comes with its own unique needs and characteristics.

• Hatchling: Bearded dragons begin their lives as tiny hatchlings, typically measuring around 3-4 inches in length. At this stage, they are extremely active and curious. Hatchlings need a high-protein diet, consisting of small insects like crickets and mealworms, as well as some vegetables and fruits. Their metabolism is fast, and they grow quickly during the first few months of life.

• Juvenile: From around 2-4 months old, a bearded dragon enters the juvenile stage, where they can grow rapidly, reaching about 8-10 inches in length. During this stage, they need a balanced diet of insects (such as crickets, dubia roaches, or silkworms) and more plant matter. As they transition from hatchlings to juveniles, their activity level remains high, and they are more likely to explore and interact with their environment. Juveniles also begin to establish their personalities, with some becoming more social and others more independent.

• Adult: Once bearded dragons reach around 12-18 months old, they are considered adults, typically ranging from 18-24 inches in length. At this stage, their growth slows significantly, and their diet becomes more balanced, with about 70% vegetables and 30% insects. Adult dragons may become less active compared to their juvenile stage but still require adequate stimulation and space to remain healthy.

2. Growth Milestones and What to Expect

As bearded dragons grow, several key milestones are important to monitor. These milestones can help you track their development and ensure they are growing at a healthy rate.

• Rapid Growth in the First Year: During the first year, bearded dragons grow quickly, reaching up to 70-80% of their adult size. You may notice them eating a lot, especially during the juvenile phase, and they should be fed high-quality food to support this rapid growth. Regular weight checks can help ensure that your dragon is gaining weight at an appropriate rate. Most hatchlings will double in size within the first few months.

• Physical Changes: Bearded dragons go through physical changes as they mature. Males typically grow larger than females and may develop more prominent features like a larger beard and brighter coloring. Around 6-12 months, males often begin to show signs of maturity, such as head-bobbing and increased territorial behavior.

• Sexual Maturity: Between 8-12 months, bearded dragons reach sexual maturity. Male dragons will start showing behaviors such as head-bobbing, beard puffing, and sometimes aggression, as they seek to establish dominance. Females may display more passive behaviors and begin the process of egg-laying once they are fully mature. If breeding is not planned, it's important to monitor these behaviors and adjust the environment accordingly to reduce stress.

3. Molting and How to Care for Your Bearded Dragon During Shedding

Molting (or shedding) is a natural part of a bearded dragon's growth process. During this phase, their skin will peel off in patches as they grow, typically occurring every few weeks, but more frequently in younger dragons.

• Signs of Shedding: Your bearded dragon may become more sluggish, less active, or appear dull in color. You might also notice patches of skin starting to peel, especially around their head, legs, and tail. This is a normal part of their growth process.

• How to Care for a Shedding Bearded Dragon: To help your dragon during shedding, ensure their habitat conditions are optimal. Humidity levels should be higher during this time (around 30-40%) to aid in shedding. You can provide a shallow dish of warm water for them to soak in, which can help soften the old skin and make it easier to shed. Avoid pulling off the skin manually, as this can cause injury. If the shedding is incomplete or seems to be causing discomfort (such as stuck skin around the toes or eyes), a vet visit may be necessary.

• Common Shedding Issues: Incomplete shedding or difficulty shedding can be a sign of dehydration, malnutrition, or other health problems. If the skin is not coming off properly or if your dragon seems to be in pain, make sure to address the issue by improving hydration, diet, or humidity levels in the habitat.

4. Managing Obesity and Ensuring Healthy Growth

Obesity is a common issue in bearded dragons, especially if their diet is not properly balanced or if they are not getting enough exercise. Managing their growth and weight is essential for their long-term health.

• Understanding Obesity: Obesity in bearded dragons can be caused by overfeeding, particularly high-fat insects, or feeding too many sugary fruits. Overweight dragons may develop joint problems, heart disease, or metabolic issues, and they will have trouble moving around, which can affect their overall quality of life.

• Feeding Guidelines: To prevent obesity, make sure to feed your bearded dragon an appropriate diet for their age and size. Hatchlings and juveniles need more protein (insects) for growth, while adults should eat mostly vegetables, with some insects included in their diet. Avoid overfeeding and provide portioned meals. Ensure that the insects fed are appropriately sized for the dragon's mouth to prevent overeating.

• Exercise and Enrichment: Bearded dragons are active creatures that need space to explore. Ensure your pet has room to roam and climb, as this helps with muscle development and overall well-being. Additionally, providing enrichment in the form of climbing structures, hiding spots, and objects to explore can help keep your dragon active and engaged.

• Monitoring Growth: Regular weight checks and monitoring your dragon's body condition will help you identify any potential weight issues early. If you notice your dragon is gaining weight too quickly or becoming lethargic, you may need to adjust their diet and exercise levels. Understanding the growth and development of your bearded dragon is crucial to providing them with the proper care throughout their life. By recognizing the different life stages, growth milestones, and shedding behaviors, you can ensure that your bearded dragon remains healthy and happy. Additionally, managing obesity and promoting healthy growth through a balanced diet and regular exercise will help keep your dragon in optimal condition as they mature.

CHAPTER THREE

BREEDING BEARDED DRAGONS

Breeding bearded dragons can be a rewarding experience, but it requires careful preparation and attention to detail. Whether you're breeding for personal interest or to sell offspring, understanding the basics of reproduction, creating a suitable breeding environment, and properly caring for the eggs and hatchlings are all essential to success.

1. The Basics of Bearded Dragon Reproduction

Bearded dragons reach sexual maturity between 8-12 months of age, though it's generally best to wait until they are around 18 months old before breeding to ensure they are fully grown and healthy.

• Mating Behavior: Male bearded dragons often display courting behaviors when they are ready to mate. This includes head-bobbing, arm waving, and puffing out their beards. Female dragons may show interest by arm waving back or showing a receptive posture, but they may also become aggressive or avoid mating if they are not ready.

• Mating Process: Once a male has courted a female successfully, the mating itself usually takes place over a series of copulations. During this time, it's important to monitor the female for signs of stress, as excessive mating can lead to exhaustion or injury. After mating, female bearded dragons can store sperm for several months, which means they can produce multiple clutches of eggs from a single mating session.

• Egg Fertilization: After successful mating, the female will start developing eggs inside her. It typically takes around 3-4 weeks for the eggs to mature before she is ready to lay them.

2. Setting Up a Breeding Environment

Creating the right environment for breeding is key to ensuring successful mating and healthy egg production. Here's how to set up the ideal breeding habitat:

• Temperature and Lighting: Bearded dragons are ectothermic (cold-blooded), meaning they rely on external heat sources to regulate their body temperature. During breeding season, it's essential to ensure that both the male and female have access to appropriate lighting and heating. UVB lighting should be used to simulate natural sunlight, which is crucial for the reproductive process. The temperature in the enclosure should range from 95-105°F (35-40°C) in the basking area, with a cooler side around 75-85°F (24-29°C).

• Enclosure Size: Provide a spacious enclosure that allows both the male and female to move around comfortably. A 75-100 gallon tank or larger is ideal for breeding pairs. The enclosure should have plenty of hiding spots and climbing opportunities to reduce stress and give the female a place to retreat if needed.

• Humidity: Proper humidity levels (around 30-40%) are essential for healthy egg development. If the humidity is too low, the eggs may not incubate properly, and if it's too high, it can cause mold or bacteria to form in the enclosure.

• Separate Enclosures for Males and Females: When not actively breeding, it's best to house males and females separately to prevent constant stress from mating attempts. You should only introduce them into the same enclosure when you're ready to begin the breeding process.

3. Caring for Eggs and Hatchlings

After mating, the female will lay her eggs, typically producing between 15 to 30 eggs per clutch. The care of these eggs and the resulting hatchlings is crucial for their survival.

• Egg Laying: Female bearded dragons dig a burrow to lay their eggs, usually in a substrate that is loose and deep enough for them to bury the eggs. Make sure the substrate is clean and offers proper burrowing conditions, such as a mix of sand, soil, and coconut fiber. After laying, she will cover the eggs and abandon them, so it's essential to gently collect the eggs and transfer them to an incubator.

• Incubation: The eggs need to be incubated at a consistent temperature of 82-88°F (28-31°C) with high humidity (about 70%). You can use an incubator specifically designed for reptile eggs, or create a DIY setup with a moist substrate and a heat source. The eggs will incubate for 55-75 days, depending on the temperature and humidity levels.

• Checking for Fertility: Before placing the eggs in the incubator, you can check for fertility by candling the eggs with a bright light. Fertile eggs will have a slight dark spot, while infertile eggs will be clear. If you notice any bad eggs, remove them immediately to prevent mold or bacteria from spreading.

• Hatching: Once the eggs hatch, baby bearded dragons (hatchlings) will emerge. Be prepared to provide them with a suitable environment for their early days. Hatchlings should be housed separately from adults to avoid aggression and ensure they have enough food and space to grow. They require the same lighting and heating as adults, but with a lower basking temperature (around 90-95°F).

4. Raising Bearded Dragon Babies: What You Need to Know

Caring for baby bearded dragons is different from caring for adults, and it's essential to meet their specific needs to ensure healthy growth and development.

• Diet: Hatchlings have very high energy needs, so their diet should primarily consist of small insects such as crickets, fruit flies, or pinhead-sized roaches, along with a small portion of finely chopped vegetables. Feed them several times a day, providing a variety of insects and greens. As they grow, you can increase the size of the insects and offer a wider variety of vegetables.

• Temperature and Lighting: Babies need proper UVB lighting to support their growth and bone development. A basking spot around 90-95°F is ideal, with a cooler side around 75-85°F. Ensure the enclosure provides plenty of hiding spots and space for the hatchlings to explore.

• Space: Bearded dragon babies are very active, and they need ample space to roam. Consider giving them a separate enclosure, at least 20 gallons for each baby, to avoid territorial stress. As they grow, they will require larger tanks.

• Health Monitoring: Regularly monitor the health of your hatchlings by checking their weight, activity level, and overall appearance. Healthy hatchlings should be active, eating well, and growing steadily. Any signs of lethargy, refusal to eat, or abnormal behavior should be addressed by a veterinarian.

5. Managing Breeding Behavior

Breeding behavior can sometimes be challenging to manage. Both male and female bearded dragons exhibit distinct behaviors during breeding season.

• Male Behavior: Males may become territorial and aggressive, particularly toward other males or females who are not receptive. They may show off their bright colors, head-bob frequently, and attempt to chase females. If multiple males are housed together, there can be frequent fighting, so it's crucial to manage them carefully.

• Female Behavior: Female bearded dragons may become aggressive or stressed during mating season, especially if they are not ready to mate. They may display defensive postures, try to escape, or refuse food. If you notice these behaviors, it may be best to separate the female from the male temporarily and allow her to rest.

• Preventing Stress: Bearded dragons can experience stress during the breeding season, especially if they are housed with incompatible tankmates or in an overcrowded environment. Provide plenty of hiding spots and ensure they have adequate food, heat, and light to minimize stress. Breeding bearded dragons can be an exciting and rewarding endeavor, but it requires careful planning and attention to detail. From setting up the breeding environment to raising healthy hatchlings, understanding the behaviors, diet, and health needs of both adults and babies will ensure success. If you're committed to providing the best care for both the parents and the offspring, breeding can result in healthy, thriving bearded dragons.

CLEANING AND MAINTENANCE OF BEARDED DRAGON HABITAT

Proper cleaning and maintenance are crucial for the health and well-being of your bearded dragon. Regular cleaning prevents the buildup of harmful bacteria, parasites, and mold, and it ensures your dragon has a safe, hygienic environment. Below are the key cleaning tasks and how to maintain a clean habitat.

1. Daily, Weekly, and Monthly Maintenance Tasks

Daily Tasks:

• Spot Clean the Enclosure: Remove any uneaten food, waste, or debris from the enclosure daily. Bearded dragons tend to have occasional accidents, so it's important to keep the tank free from any droppings. Check for any wet spots or soiled areas in the substrate and clean them immediately.

• Inspect Water Dish: Make sure your bearded dragon's water dish is clean and filled with fresh, clean water every day. Water should be changed daily to prevent bacteria growth.

• Check Temperature and Humidity: Use a thermometer and hygrometer to check the temperature and humidity levels inside the enclosure. Ensure that the basking area is warm enough and the cooler side is at the right temperature, and that the humidity stays at optimal levels.

Weekly Tasks:

• Full Habitat Cleaning: Once a week, perform a more thorough cleaning by removing all decorations, logs, and rocks from the enclosure. Scrub these items with a reptile-safe disinfectant or a mild soap and rinse them thoroughly. Let them dry completely before putting them back into the tank.

• Clean the Substrate: If you're using loose substrates (e.g., sand, reptile carpet), clean them weekly by removing any visible droppings and replacing any soiled substrate. If you use a loose substrate, avoid using anything that can easily be ingested by your bearded dragon, as this can cause impaction.

• Inspect Fixtures: Check the lighting and heating fixtures weekly to ensure they are functioning properly. Look for any signs of wear, breakage, or burnt-out bulbs that may need replacing.

Monthly Tasks:

• Deep Clean the Enclosure: Once a month, deep clean the entire habitat. Remove all the substrate, decorations, and furniture. Clean and disinfect all surfaces inside the enclosure, including walls and the floor. Use a reptile-safe cleaner to wipe down the entire tank, rinse well, and dry thoroughly.

• Check for Wear on Lighting and Heating Fixtures: Ensure that the UVB bulbs are still providing the proper amount of UV radiation (they typically need to be replaced every 6-12 months). Check your basking light and heat source to ensure they are maintaining the right temperatures.

• Check for Pests or Parasites: Examine your bearded dragon closely for signs of mites, parasites, or other health issues. It's important to inspect your tank for any signs of pests, and if you spot any, treat the enclosure immediately.

2. Cleaning the Habitat: Keeping It Hygienic and Safe

Keeping the habitat clean is key to maintaining a healthy environment for your bearded dragon. Here's how to keep the habitat hygienic:

• Disinfecting the Tank: When cleaning the tank, avoid using harsh chemicals like bleach. Instead, use a reptile-safe disinfectant or create a DIY solution using vinegar and water to wipe down surfaces. Vinegar is effective at killing bacteria and mold while being safe for your pet.

• Handling Waste: Immediately remove any feces from the enclosure to prevent bacteria build-up. Bearded dragons often defecate in one or two spots, so it's easier to clean the waste regularly. If there is an accidental mess in the substrate, remove the affected area and replace it with fresh material.

• Removing Old Food: After offering food, remove any leftovers after an hour or two, as spoiled food can quickly rot and attract pests. Vegetables can wilt quickly, and insects can leave waste, so it's essential to remove uneaten food promptly.

• Cleaning Decorations: Regularly clean all the decorations, logs, rocks, and hiding spots in the tank. These can accumulate waste and bacteria, so washing them weekly or bi-weekly ensures a clean environment.

3. Maintaining Proper Lighting and Heating Fixtures

Bearded dragons need proper lighting and heating to thrive. Regular maintenance of these fixtures is essential to ensure your dragon's health.

• UVB Lighting: Bearded dragons require UVB lighting for 10-12 hours a day to synthesize vitamin D3, which helps them absorb calcium. Replace UVB bulbs every 6-12 months, even if they still appear to be working. Over time, the UVB radiation output decreases, even if the bulb is still on.

• Basking Light: The basking light should maintain a temperature between 95-105°F (35-40°C). Regularly check the temperature with a thermometer to ensure it's within the proper range. You should also replace basking bulbs that are not providing enough heat or light.

• Night Temperature: At night, the enclosure should cool down to a temperature between 65-75°F (18-24°C). Be sure to monitor the temperatures with a reliable thermometer, and avoid using heat lamps at night, as bearded dragons need a clear day/night cycle to stay healthy.

• Cleaning Fixtures: Lighting and heating fixtures should be checked for dirt, dust, or debris that might block heat or UVB rays. Clean the bulbs gently with a dry cloth to remove dust and ensure they continue to work effectively.

4. Dealing with Common Problems: Odors, Mites, and Bacteria

Certain problems may arise in the enclosure that can be addressed with regular cleaning and care.

Odors:

• Cause: Odors are often caused by uneaten food, waste, or dirty water. Improper ventilation can also lead to unpleasant smells.

• Solution: Clean the tank regularly and remove any uneaten food or waste immediately. Ensure proper ventilation in the tank, and consider using a small fan if needed to promote air circulation. Also, maintain a regular cleaning schedule to prevent odors from building up.

Mites:

• Cause: Mites can infest your bearded dragon's enclosure if not regularly cleaned. These tiny pests can cause irritation, itching, and discomfort for your pet.

• Solution: If you spot mites, remove all decorations, clean the tank thoroughly, and replace the substrate. Mite infestations may require a visit to the vet for treatment, and you may need to treat the enclosure with a reptile-safe mite solution.

Bacteria:

• Cause: Bacteria can thrive in dirty environments, especially in areas with leftover food or feces. This can lead to infections or other health issues.

• Solution: Regularly clean the habitat to remove waste, uneaten food, and debris. Ensure that your bearded dragon's water dish is cleaned daily, and that any areas where bacteria may thrive are disinfected regularly. Maintaining a clean and well-maintained habitat is crucial for the health and longevity of your bearded dragon. By following daily, weekly, and monthly cleaning routines, ensuring proper lighting and heating, and dealing with common issues such as odors, mites, and bacteria, you will create a safe and comfortable environment for your pet to thrive in. Regular maintenance and a vigilant approach to cleanliness are key components of responsible bearded dragon care.

TRAVELING WITH YOUR BEARDED DRAGON A GUIDE TO SAFE JOURNEYS

Traveling with your bearded dragon can be a rewarding experience, but it requires careful preparation to ensure their safety and comfort during the journey. Whether you're going on a road trip or taking a flight, understanding how to properly transport your pet and help them adjust to new environments is key to reducing stress and keeping them healthy. Below is a comprehensive guide to help you navigate traveling with your bearded dragon.

1. Preparing for Travel: What to Pack and How to Transport

Before embarking on your trip, proper preparation is essential to ensure that your bearded dragon has everything they need while you're away from home. Here's what to pack and how to transport your pet safely:

Essential Items to Pack:

• Transport Carrier: Choose a well-ventilated, secure, and appropriately sized carrier for your bearded dragon. It should have enough space for your pet to move around but still feel secure. A small, sturdy box or a reptile-specific travel carrier works well.

• Temperature Control: Keep a thermometer with you to monitor your bearded dragon's environment. Depending on the length of your journey, you may need a portable heat pack or cooling pack to maintain proper temperatures.

• Water Dish: Bearded dragons need access to fresh water at all times. Bring along a portable water container and a dish for them to drink from. You can also bring a spray bottle to lightly mist them and keep them hydrated.

• Food and Treats: Pack enough food for the trip, including vegetables, fruits, and insects. Carry a small cooler if you're traveling with perishable foods.

• Bedding or Substrate: Place a soft layer of paper towels or non-toxic reptile bedding in the carrier to provide comfort and absorb waste.

• First Aid Kit: Carry a basic reptile first aid kit with you in case of emergencies. It should include antiseptic wipes, gauze, and any medication your bearded dragon might need.

2. Tips for Safe Car Travel

Car travel can be one of the most straightforward ways to transport your bearded dragon, but safety and comfort are still important. Follow these tips to ensure a smooth trip:

• Secure the Carrier: Always secure the carrier in your vehicle to prevent it from sliding or tipping over during the drive. It's best to place the carrier on the floor or the back seat, away from any direct sunlight or drafts.

• Keep the Temperature Consistent: Avoid letting the car get too hot or too cold. Your bearded dragon needs a stable temperature between 75-85°F (24-29°C) for comfort. Use portable heat packs in cooler weather, and avoid leaving the vehicle in direct sunlight during hot weather.

• Avoid Stressful Situations: If possible, limit loud noises, sudden stops, or excessive motion, as these can stress your bearded dragon. Keep the ride as calm and smooth as possible.

• Frequent Breaks: For longer trips, stop every 1-2 hours to check on your bearded dragon and offer water if necessary. This will help reduce any discomfort from being in the carrier for extended periods.

• Never Leave in the Car: Never leave your bearded dragon alone in a parked car, especially in warm weather. Cars can heat up quickly, creating dangerous conditions for your pet.

3. Flying with Your Bearded Dragon: What to Know

Flying with a bearded dragon is more complex than car travel, but it's still possible with the right planning. Here's what to keep in mind:

• Check Airline Policies: Before booking your flight, check with the airline to see if they allow pets, and if so, what their policies are for traveling with reptiles. Some airlines may not permit reptiles in the cabin, while others allow them as carry-on luggage.

• Travel Carrier Regulations: Ensure that the carrier meets airline regulations for size and ventilation. It should be large enough for your bearded dragon to turn around comfortably but small enough to fit under the seat in front of you (if traveling in-cabin).

• Keep Calm and Secure: Avoid taking your bearded dragon out of the carrier during the flight. Stress can make the experience harder for them, and there are risks of injury or escape. Keep the carrier covered with a towel or blanket to help reduce visual stimuli.

• Pre-Flight Preparation: Before your flight, keep your bearded dragon well-fed and hydrated, but avoid feeding them immediately before the trip to reduce the risk of motion sickness. Take them to the vet for a checkup if you're concerned about the stresses of flying.

4. Settling In After Travel: Reducing Stress

Once you arrive at your destination, it's important to help your bearded dragon adjust to their new surroundings and reduce stress. Here are some tips for settling them in:

• Create a Familiar Environment: As soon as you arrive, try to replicate your bearded dragon's regular habitat as much as possible. Set up their enclosure with familiar items such as logs, rocks, and a substrate they recognize. Having a space that feels familiar can help them feel more comfortable.

• Provide Quiet and Calm: Bearded dragons can easily become stressed in noisy or chaotic environments. Give them some quiet time to acclimate to the new space. Keep handling to a minimum for the first few hours or days, depending on how they react.

• Maintain Proper Heating and Lighting: Be sure to set up their basking area and UVB lighting as close as possible to their home setup. This will help them feel at ease and prevent disruptions to their normal behavior.

• Hydrate and Feed: Offer water and food shortly after arrival to help them rehydrate and recover from the journey. If they don't eat right away, don't worry. It's common for reptiles to experience a little temporary loss of appetite after travel.

• Observe Behavior: Watch for any signs of stress or discomfort, such as lethargy, refusal to eat, or excessive hiding. If you notice unusual behavior, consult a vet to rule out health concerns. Traveling with a bearded dragon requires thoughtful preparation and care. Whether you're taking a road trip or flying to a new destination, you can make the experience as stress-free as possible by packing the essentials, keeping their environment comfortable, and monitoring their well-being. By following these guidelines and taking extra precautions during and after the trip, you'll ensure that your bearded dragon remains safe, healthy, and content throughout the journey.

CHAPTER FOUR

COMMON PROBLEMS AND TROUBLESHOOTING FOR BEARDED DRAGONS

Bearded dragons are relatively low-maintenance pets, but like any animal, they can experience health or behavioral issues. It's important to address these problems early to ensure your pet remains healthy and happy. Below are some of the most common problems owners encounter, along with troubleshooting tips on how to manage them.

1. How to Deal with Loss of Appetite

Loss of appetite in bearded dragons can occur for various reasons, including stress, illness, improper diet, or environmental issues. If your bearded dragon refuses to eat, it's important to identify the root cause and take action.

Troubleshooting:

• Check Temperature and Lighting: Ensure that the temperature in their enclosure is appropriate, with a basking area around 100-110°F (38-43°C) and a cooler side around 75-85°F (24-29°C). Also, ensure they are receiving proper UVB lighting.

• Provide a Variety of Food: Bearded dragons may become bored with their diet. Offer a mix of greens (like collard greens or mustard greens), fruits (such as strawberries or mangoes), and live insects (crickets or mealworms). Ensure that the food is fresh and appropriately sized.

• Minimize Stress: Excessive handling or changes to their environment can cause stress, leading to a loss of appetite. Make sure their habitat is quiet and calm, and avoid too much interaction until they start eating again.

• Check for Illness: If the loss of appetite lasts for more than a few days, or if they show other signs of illness (like weight loss, lethargy, or changes in stool), a trip to the vet is essential.

2. What to Do if Your Bearded Dragon Is Lethargic

Lethargy, or a noticeable lack of energy, can signal a variety of issues, including improper temperature, stress, or health problems such as parasites or metabolic bone disease.

Troubleshooting:

• Check Environmental Conditions: Ensure that your bearded dragon's enclosure has the correct temperature gradient (75-85°F for the cooler side, 100-110°F for the basking area). Poor lighting, particularly a lack of UVB light, can also lead to lethargy.

• Consider Diet: If your bearded dragon isn't getting enough of the right nutrients, they may become lethargic. Ensure that you are offering a balanced diet, including both greens and insects, and supplementing with calcium and vitamin D3 if necessary.

• Hydration: Dehydration can cause lethargy. Make sure your bearded dragon has access to clean water at all times and offer moist greens or mist them lightly with water if they are not drinking enough.

• Look for Illness: If lethargy persists for several days, along with other symptoms like vomiting, diarrhea, or swelling, it may indicate a health issue. A visit to the vet is recommended for a proper diagnosis.

3. Addressing Aggression and Territorial Behavior

Bearded dragons are typically calm, but they can exhibit aggression or territorial behavior, especially during breeding season or when they feel threatened.

Troubleshooting:

• Avoid Overcrowding: If you have more than one bearded dragon, ensure that they have enough space. Male bearded dragons are particularly territorial, and fights can occur if they feel crowded. Separate any aggressive individuals into their own enclosures.

• Handling and Socialization: Frequent and gentle handling from a young age helps reduce fear and aggression. Always approach your bearded dragon calmly and avoid sudden movements.

• Breeding Season Behavior: During breeding season, males can become more territorial and aggressive. This is a natural instinct, and it may be necessary to separate them from females or other males during this time.

• Provide Hiding Spots: Bearded dragons may become aggressive if they feel exposed or stressed. Ensure that their enclosure has plenty of hiding spots where they can retreat when they feel overwhelmed.

4. Managing Weight Issues: Underweight and Overweight Dragons

Maintaining a healthy weight is essential for your bearded dragon's well-being. Both being underweight and overweight can lead to health problems.

Troubleshooting:

• Underweight Bearded Dragon:

Ensure Proper Diet: Feed your bearded dragon a balanced diet with the right proportion of greens, fruits, and protein (insects). Offer high-calcium foods, like collard greens, and consider dusting their food with calcium powder to support growth.

Increase Meal Frequency: If your bearded dragon is underweight, consider offering food more frequently, including insects that are higher in protein, such as crickets and mealworms.

Visit the Vet: If your bearded dragon continues to lose weight despite a proper diet, there may be an underlying health issue. A vet visit is important to rule out parasites or metabolic disorders.

• Overweight Bearded Dragon:

Limit High-Fat Foods: Avoid overfeeding high-fat insects like superworms or fatty fruits, and reduce the frequency of feeding. Focus on offering a variety of vegetables and limit treats.

Proper Exercise: Provide opportunities for your bearded dragon to roam outside their enclosure and explore, which will help them stay active and burn off excess calories.

Vet Consultation: If your bearded dragon becomes overweight, it's essential to consult with a vet. Excess weight can lead to health complications such as fatty liver disease or joint problems.

5. How to Handle Behavioral or Environmental Stress

Stress can lead to a range of problems, including loss of appetite, lethargy, aggression, and even health issues. Identifying the cause of stress is essential in helping your bearded dragon recover.

Troubleshooting:

• Review Environmental Factors: Ensure that the enclosure is not too small, overly hot, or too cold. Stress can occur if the bearded dragon's habitat doesn't mimic the conditions of their natural environment. Make sure that there's a proper temperature gradient, UVB lighting, and enough space for your pet.

• Minimize Handling: Bearded dragons can get stressed from excessive handling, particularly in new environments or during changes in routine.

Limit handling to a few minutes each day, especially during periods of adjustment.

• Avoid Sudden Changes: Bearded dragons are creatures of habit. Sudden changes, such as moving their enclosure or introducing new animals, can cause stress. Introduce changes gradually, and always provide familiar hiding spots to make them feel secure.

• Monitor for Health Issues: If you notice ongoing stress symptoms, such as changes in behavior or eating habits, it could be linked to health problems. A visit to the vet can help determine if illness is a factor. Bearded dragons are generally hardy pets, but like any animal, they can experience common health or behavioral issues. By identifying potential problems early, whether it's loss of appetite, aggression, or stress, you can address them quickly and keep your pet happy and healthy. Regular maintenance of their habitat, a balanced diet, and proper handling techniques are key to preventing these issues from arising. If symptoms persist or worsen, seeking advice from a veterinarian is always a prudent step.

BEARDED DRAGON ENRICHMENT AND MENTAL STIMULATION

Just like any other pet, bearded dragons require more than just food, water, and a warm, safe environment. Mental stimulation is essential for their well-being, as it helps keep them active, curious, and happy. Providing enrichment encourages natural behaviors, such as exploring, climbing, and hunting, which can reduce boredom, stress, and even destructive habits.

1. The Importance of Mental Stimulation for Bearded Dragons

Mental stimulation is vital for the overall health and happiness of bearded dragons. In the wild, they engage in a variety of behaviors such as hunting for food, exploring their environment, and interacting with other creatures. Without proper mental engagement, bearded dragons can become bored, stressed, or depressed, which can lead to health issues and behavioral problems.

Key Benefits of Mental Stimulation:

• Reduced Stress: A mentally engaged dragon is less likely to become stressed or anxious, which can lead to better physical health and a longer life.

• Increased Activity: Regular stimulation encourages exercise, which helps maintain a healthy weight and supports their natural instincts.

• Improved Digestion: As they "hunt" for food or explore new objects, they experience a more natural feeding behavior, which can support healthy digestion.

• Preventing Boredom: Boredom is one of the leading causes of behavioral issues. Mental stimulation offers new challenges and experiences for your bearded dragon to enjoy.

2. Enrichment Ideas: Toys, Climbing Structures, and More

Providing a variety of enrichment activities is essential for keeping your bearded dragon engaged. You don't need to go overboard with expensive toys; many enrichment ideas can be created with items you may already have at home.

Enrichment Ideas for Your Bearded Dragon:

• Climbing Structures: Bearded dragons love to climb and perch on high spots. Adding logs, rocks, branches, or specially designed reptile hammocks to their habitat can create a vertical space that encourages climbing and exploration.

• Hiding Spots: Provide areas where your bearded dragon can hide, such as caves, tunnels, or piles of rocks. Hiding helps them feel secure, and it also encourages natural behaviors like burrowing or seeking shelter.

• Interactive Toys: Though bearded dragons are not as playful as some other pets, they can still enjoy chasing and interacting with simple toys. For example, you can try rolling a small ball or piece of paper for them to chase. Some pet stores sell reptile-friendly toys designed to stimulate their natural instincts.

• Food foraging: Hide their food in different parts of the enclosure to encourage foraging behavior. You can scatter veggies, crickets, or mealworms in various places within their habitat or place them inside safe food puzzle toys.

• Live Plants: Adding safe, non-toxic plants to their enclosure can provide both enrichment and a more natural habitat. Some plants may encourage climbing or provide hiding spots, while others simply give your bearded dragon something new to interact with.

3. Creating a Dynamic Habitat to Keep Your Dragon Engaged

A dynamic habitat is a key aspect of bearded dragon enrichment. By creating an environment that mimics their natural habitat, you can help your pet feel more at home and engaged.

Tips for Creating a Dynamic Habitat:

• Varied Terrain: Include a mix of textures and surfaces in the enclosure, such as rocks, wood, branches, and soil. This variety not only gives your bearded dragon more to explore but also helps mimic their natural surroundings, where they would climb, dig, and bask.

• Basking and Cooling Zones: Set up clear temperature gradients within the enclosure, with a hot basking area and a cooler retreat space. Allowing your bearded dragon to choose their preferred temperature zone can help them feel more in control and reduce stress.

• Rotate Decorations and Objects: Changing the layout of the habitat periodically can help stimulate your bearded dragon's curiosity and reduce monotony. You don't have to do this frequently, but occasional rearrangement can make the enclosure feel like a new environment.

• Varied Lighting and UVB Exposure: Ensuring your bearded dragon gets appropriate lighting and UVB exposure is essential for their health and well-being. UVB light helps them synthesize vitamin D3, which is crucial for calcium absorption and bone health. Using a combination of natural light and artificial UVB can create a dynamic environment that mimics day-night cycles.

4. Benefits of Interaction and Social Time

While bearded dragons are solitary creatures by nature, they still benefit from regular interaction with their human caregivers. Social time helps build trust, reduce stress, and offer mental stimulation.

Benefits of Interaction:

• Building Trust: Regular, gentle handling helps your bearded dragon become accustomed to human interaction. With time, they can learn to trust you and may even seek out attention, though it's important to allow them to approach you on their terms.

• Exercise: When allowed to roam outside their enclosure, bearded dragons can engage in more exercise, such as exploring new environments. Supervised free-roaming sessions are great for stimulating their curiosity and giving them the chance to hunt for food or bask in different areas.

• Bonding Time: Although bearded dragons may not be as affectionate as some pets, many owners report that their dragons enjoy sitting on their laps or perching on their shoulders. This bonding time allows them to relax and feel safe in your presence.

How to Interact with Your Bearded Dragon:

• Handle them gently and calmly, and avoid sudden movements that could startle them.

• Provide a consistent daily routine to minimize stress.

• Take them out for supervised time outside their enclosure in a safe, enclosed space where they can explore.

Mental stimulation and enrichment are just as important for your bearded dragon as their physical health. By providing a dynamic habitat, incorporating interactive toys, and engaging with them regularly, you can ensure that your bearded dragon remains happy, healthy, and mentally sharp. A well-stimulated bearded dragon will lead a more fulfilling life, with reduced stress and better overall well-being. So, take the time to offer them opportunities for exploration, play, and bonding to keep them mentally engaged and active.

ETHICAL OWNERSHIP AND BEARDED DRAGON CONSERVATION

Owning a bearded dragon can be an incredibly rewarding experience, but it also comes with the responsibility to ensure their well-being and contribute to their conservation. As a pet owner, it's essential to be mindful of the ethical implications of owning and caring for a bearded dragon. From understanding the responsibilities of responsible pet ownership to supporting efforts that protect these creatures in the wild, ethical ownership is vital for their welfare.

1. The Importance of Responsible Pet Ownership

Responsible pet ownership means more than simply providing the basic needs of food, water, and shelter. It involves understanding the specific needs of bearded dragons, creating a safe and enriching environment, and ensuring their long-term well-being.

Key Aspects of Responsible Pet Ownership:

• Commitment to Care: Bearded dragons can live for 10-15 years, so owning one requires a long-term commitment. It's essential to ensure that your dragon's needs are met for their entire lifespan, including appropriate housing, nutrition, and health care.

• Proper Habitat: Creating an appropriate living space that meets your dragon's physical and behavioral needs is crucial. This includes providing a temperature gradient, UVB lighting, safe substrates, and enrichment opportunities.

• Health and Veterinary Care: Regular check-ups with a qualified reptile vet can help detect health issues early. Providing proper nutrition, supplements, and hydration is essential for your bearded dragon's health.

• Respecting Their Nature: Bearded dragons are solitary creatures that require periods of solitude and quiet. Being aware of their natural behaviors and giving them space when they need it is part of being a responsible pet owner.

2. Legal Considerations: Ensuring Compliance with Local Laws

Before acquiring a bearded dragon, it's important to familiarize yourself with any legal regulations regarding the ownership of exotic pets in your area. Different regions may have specific rules related to the breeding, trade, and care of bearded dragons, particularly when it comes to wild-caught versus captive-bred dragons.

Legal Considerations:

• Captive-Bred vs. Wild-Caught: In many places, it is illegal to capture and sell wild bearded dragons. Pet owners should ensure that their pet is sourced from reputable breeders who focus on captive breeding programs that do not negatively impact wild populations.

• Permits and Licenses: Some states or countries require permits to keep exotic animals. Research local laws and obtain any necessary permits before acquiring a bearded dragon.

• Wildlife Protection Laws: In some regions, bearded dragons are considered protected species, and it's illegal to harvest them from the wild. Ensuring that your dragon comes from a legal, ethical source is essential to avoiding contributing to illegal wildlife trafficking.

3. Supporting Bearded Dragon Conservation Efforts in the Wild

While captive breeding has helped decrease the demand for wild-caught bearded dragons, conservation efforts to protect wild populations are still crucial. In their natural habitat, bearded dragons face threats from habitat destruction, illegal poaching, and climate change.

Ways to Support Conservation Efforts:

• Support Reputable Breeders: Purchase bearded dragons from breeders who are committed to ethical practices, including maintaining genetic diversity and ensuring that no harm is done to wild populations.

• Donate to Conservation Organizations: Contribute to or volunteer with organizations that are working to protect bearded dragons and other reptile species in the wild. These groups often work on projects that focus on habitat preservation, anti-poaching efforts, and scientific research.

• Spread Awareness: Educating others about the importance of responsible pet ownership and conservation can help reduce the demand for wild-caught animals and promote the ethical treatment of reptiles.

• Research and Learn: Stay informed about conservation issues affecting bearded dragons. Understanding their role in the ecosystem and the challenges they face can help you become a more responsible advocate for their protection.

4. The Impact of the Pet Trade on Wild Populations

The pet trade, while largely made up of ethically bred and cared-for animals, has historically had a negative impact on wild populations of many species, including bearded dragons. Harvesting wild bearded dragons for the pet trade can deplete natural populations, disrupt ecosystems, and contribute to the decline of species in certain regions.

Key Impacts of the Pet Trade:

• Overexploitation: In some areas, the demand for wild-caught bearded dragons has led to overexploitation, which can harm the natural population and cause declines in local ecosystems.

• Habitat Destruction: The collection of wild animals often goes hand in hand with habitat destruction. As more animals are removed from their natural habitats, it can lead to significant ecological damage.

• Genetic Bottlenecks: Wild populations removed from their natural environment and bred in captivity may experience genetic bottlenecks, reducing their genetic diversity and overall health.

Ways to Minimize Impact:

• Buy Only from Ethical Breeders: Ensure that you are purchasing a bearded dragon from a reputable breeder who only produces animals that were bred in captivity. This helps reduce the demand for wild-caught reptiles.

• Advocate for Sustainable Practices: Support policies and organizations that promote sustainable practices in the pet trade, such as those that regulate the capture and trade of wild reptiles.

• Educate Others: Encourage others to consider adopting or purchasing from breeders who are committed to ethical breeding practices rather than acquiring wild-caught bearded dragons.

Ethical ownership and conservation of bearded dragons are vital components of responsible pet care. By committing to responsible ownership, ensuring compliance with local laws, supporting conservation efforts, and being mindful of the impact of the pet trade, we can all play a part in ensuring the well-being of both captive and wild populations of bearded dragons. Understanding and embracing our responsibility as pet owners is not only beneficial for the animals we care for but also for preserving the natural habitats and ecosystems in which these incredible creatures thrive.

FINAL TIPS FOR BEARDED DRAGON CARE

• Monitor Health Regularly: Always keep an eye on your dragon's behavior and health. If you notice any signs of illness, such as changes in appetite, lethargy, or abnormal behavior, consult a vet right away.

• Provide Proper Lighting and Heating: Bearded dragons need a UVB light for calcium absorption and proper heat regulation. Make sure you provide a temperature gradient with a basking spot and cooler areas in their habitat.

• Offer a Varied Diet: A balanced diet that includes vegetables, fruits, and insects is essential for their growth and health. Be sure to provide fresh food daily and avoid overfeeding or underfeeding.

• Respect Their Space: Bearded dragons are solitary creatures. While they may enjoy socializing with their owners, they also need time to themselves to rest and feel secure.

LONG-TERM COMMITMENT AND LIFESPAN EXPECTATIONS

Bearded dragons can live anywhere from 10 to 15 years with proper care, and in some cases, even longer. This means that owning a bearded dragon is a significant long-term commitment, requiring you to plan for their care, health, and well-being over many years.

• Lifespan Expectations: Bearded dragons have a relatively long lifespan compared to many other reptiles. As they age, their care needs may change, including dietary adjustments, more frequent vet checkups, and changes in their activity levels.

• Plan for Their Future: Always be prepared for the evolving needs of your dragon as they grow from hatchlings to adults. They will need larger enclosures, more space, and different heating requirements as they mature.

CONTINUING EDUCATION FOR BEARDED DRAGON OWNERS

The world of reptile care is constantly evolving, and as a bearded dragon owner, it's important to stay updated on the latest care techniques, health information, and enrichment ideas. Continuing your education will help you provide the best possible care for your dragon and ensure their long-term happiness.

• Read and Research: Stay informed by reading books, articles, and joining online communities or forums dedicated to bearded dragons. Connecting with other owners and experts can provide valuable tips and advice.

• Attend Reptile Care Classes or Events: Many reptile shops, pet expos, or veterinary clinics offer classes or events where you can learn more about bearded dragon care, health issues, and breeding.

• Consult Experts: When in doubt, consult with a qualified reptile veterinarian who can offer professional guidance on all aspects of bearded dragon care.

By staying dedicated to their needs, being aware of the responsibilities, and seeking out additional knowledge, you can ensure your bearded dragon enjoys a long, healthy, and happy life.

Conclusion

Caring for a bearded dragon is a rewarding experience that requires dedication, knowledge, and long-term commitment. From providing the right habitat and diet to ensuring their physical and mental well-being, your bearded dragon relies on you to meet their needs for a fulfilling life. As a responsible pet owner, it's important to stay informed, adapt your care routine as your dragon grows, and be mindful of the impact of your actions on both the animal and the environment.